AF725838

Cordelia Williams is a barrister at Pump Court Chambers who specialises in financial remedies and private law children matters. She is regularly instructed in complex disputes, often appearing against senior barristers of leading family chambers. She is listed in The Legal 500 2024 as a 'Rising Star' (Tier 1).

Claire Howard is a senior associate solicitor and mediator at Rayden Solicitors. She is a Law Society Family Law Panel Member specialising in relationship breakdowns for married and unmarried couples, and where children are involved. Claire is experienced in progressing proceedings through alternative dispute resolution including mediation and arbitration.

A Practical Guide to Remarriage and Divorce

A Practical Guide to Remarriage and Divorce

Cordelia Williams

Barrister

MA (Hons) LLM

Claire Howard

Solicitor and Mediator

LLB (Hons)

Law Brief Publishing

© Cordelia Williams & Claire Howard

All rights reserved. No part of this publication may be reproduced, stored in a retrieval system, or transmitted, in any form or by any means, electronic, mechanical, photocopying, recording or otherwise, without the prior permission of the publisher.

Excerpts from judgments and statutes are Crown copyright. Any Crown Copyright material is reproduced with the permission of the Controller of OPSI and the King's Printer for Scotland. Some quotations may be licensed under the terms of the Open Government Licence (http://www.nationalarchives.gov.uk/doc/open-government-licence/version/3). Some of the material used in this publication was first published in 'Remarriage: Avoiding the Elephant Trap', Financial Remedies Journal 2023 Issue 3 Winter, 208-211 and is reproduced with Class Legal's kind permission.

Cover image © iStockphoto.com/Denym Taylor

The information in this book was believed to be correct at the time of writing. All content is for information purposes only and is not intended as legal advice. No liability is accepted by either the publisher or author for any errors or omissions (whether negligent or not) that it may contain. Professional advice should always be obtained before applying any information to particular circumstances.

Published 2024 by Law Brief Publishing, an imprint of Law Brief Publishing Ltd
30 The Parks
Minehead
Somerset
TA24 8BT

www.lawbriefpublishing.com

Paperback: 978-1-916698-43-7

FOREWORD

As family practitioners, we are usually more concerned about dealing with the fallout from marriage breakdown – protective measures, the arrangements for the children, financial settlements – that we often overlook the practicalities of how and when the marriage itself is brought to an end.

From time to time, a case will be reported which not only demonstrates just how important it is to ensure that the decree proceedings themselves are given proper consideration, but which will also strike fear in the heart of any divorce practitioner. In *K v K (Financial Remedy: Final Order Prior to Decree Nisi)* [2017] 1 FLR 541, it was discovered some months after the contested final financial hearing that there had been no decree nisi in place when the final order was made. The final order was declared a nullity and the parties were back to where they started. More recently, practitioners had their heads in their hands reading *Williams v Williams* [2024] EWHC 733 (Fam), in which the President of the Family Division determined that a solicitor's erroneous click of a mouse brought a marriage to an end prematurely and (as far as Mr and Mrs Williams were concerned, unexpectedly) with potentially far-reaching and expensive consequences.

For divorce practitioners, therefore, as much attention will be paid to the practicalities of bringing the marriage to an end as it is to finalising the financial arrangements. In the usual case, before closing a divorce file, solicitors will ensure that not only has the final divorce order been made, but the financial consent order has been approved and clients are sent away with clear information about the consequences of remarriage on the financial arrangements they have made.

However, we know from the '*Fair Shares? Sorting out money and property on divorce*" report (Hitchings, Bryson, Douglas, Burdon, Birchall: November 2023) that in 52% of the cases surveyed, couples sorted out their own financial arrangements without any legal help. Even more worryingly, in over a third of cases (36%) no financial arrangements were made at all.

When I was working as a very junior solicitor in the late 1990s, often the most difficult cases were those in which clients sought to finalise financial arrangements many years after their divorce, during which time their personal lives had changed dramatically, as had the overall financial landscape. It was drummed into us junior practitioners that the first question to be asked in those circumstances was always 'have you or your ex-spouse remarried?' because, as Cordelia and Claire explain in this book, the consequences for those who have remarried in the intervening period can be catastrophic.

This is not an easy area of law and the answers are not easy to find. We know of the 'elephant trap' into which some clients may fall inadvertently if they remarry before resolving financial arrangements with their previous spouse but remain unclear about when it applies. There remain misconceptions, even amongst senior, experienced practitioners. At the Resolution Conference in May 2024, it was clear from questions asked in an open forum that not all practitioners understood that, when it comes to remarriage and the 'elephant trap', pension sharing falls into a category of its own. Acting Deemster Horton KC's recent decision in the Isle of Man case of *Hyslop v Hyslop* 2DS 2022/13 & 2DS 2023/03 adds yet a further layer of complex analysis about when a 'piggy-back' claim might be made by the remarried spouse falling into such a trap.

Cordelia and Claire's excellent book is therefore as timely as it is important. It explains in clear and simple terms the consequences of remarriage, what the 'elephant trap' is and how to avoid it and, importantly, how to extricate a client from it when things have gone wrong. It is recommended reading for every divorce practitioner – you are likely to need it more often than you might expect.

Samantha Hillas KC
June 2024

PREFACE

It has been 16 years since the late Singer J coined the pithy term of the 'elephant trap' of premature remarriage in the case of *E v E* [2008] 1 FLR 220. This area of law remains surprisingly legally neglected despite the unfortunately common approach of divorcees putting off the finalisation of their financial arrangements.

Over the years there has been wider commentary and judicial intervention addressing the importance of timing and application-type in cases of premature remarriage. Common issues are addressed in this book, together with analysis of recent case law where a remarried party attempts to 'piggy-back' off an unmarried party's claim, and where there may be a competing claim from another former spouse.

This book also explores alternative claims in circumstances of premature remarriage to help practitioners advise a client who has been elephant-trapped, together with which applications may be appropriate and/or what to look for when advising a remarried or remarrying party.

We are very grateful to Samantha Hillas KC for kindly contributing her thoughts in the foreword. She is a particularly knowledgeable commentator given her involvement with *Hyslop v Hyslop* 2DS 2022/13 & 2DS 2023/03.

The authors believe that the law is stated as of 1 July 2024.

Cordelia Williams
Claire Howard
July 2024

CONTENTS

INTRODUCTION

The topic of remarriage is often one that rears its head for practitioners in time-pressured, stressful circumstances. Commonly, this is when a client seeks advice on the brink of a remarriage, to 'check' that 'there are no issues' hanging over from their previous marriage. This book is designed to help practitioners in exactly that arresting circumstance. To ensure timely and accurate advice is given, before clients haplessly fall into another marriage without their eyes being fully open as to the consequences.

It can take some divorces several months and even years to conclude. This is not always a result of hostility or acrimony. It can be due to complex assets or waiting for those assets to reach their true values before determining the appropriate division. Whilst enduring such delays, it is not uncommon for parties to meet new partners and want to move forwards with their lives; that can sometimes result in their remarriage.

Statistics confirm that remarriage is common. 22.6% of men and 21.3% of women entering into opposite-sex marriages have been previously married. For same-sex marriages, the numbers are lower: 11% of men and 19% of women have been previously married; albeit this statistic is likely skewed by the relatively more recent introduction of same-sex marriages.

As per the latest Office for National Statistics ('ONS') information, 'the most common age range for a man to remarry in 2022 was aged 60 to 69'. For women, the most common age range to remarry is aged 50 to 54 years, and remarrying women are more likely than remarrying men to have been divorced rather than widowed. (ONS marriages in England and Wales: 2021 and 2022).

Timely legal advice is both prudent and essential to preserve a remarrying party's legitimate financial claims before they are dismissed. Failure for those parties to obtain legal advice prior to making such significant decisions can lead to a catastrophic outcome, forfeiting genuine financial claims. It is crucial that clients understand that their remarrying can sacrifice more than their former relationship.

In circumstances where a client has remarried despite advice to the contrary, or indeed without having sought advice beforehand, this book also examines its effect on their financial claims subject to the timings and applications made, and the impact of their remarriage on the former spouse's claims who has not remarried.

We will firstly set out and explain the legal consequences of a second (/third/fourth/fifth etc.) marriage. This is the foundation of advice for clients to avoid falling into the 'elephant trap' of a premature remarriage. 'Elephant trap' is the pithy term coined by the late Singer J, in the case of *E v E* [2008] 1 FLR 220, detailed further below.

Thereafter, we will explore possible legal and procedural alternatives available to clients who have already remarried, together with their risks and merits.

It is a messy and somewhat legally neglected topic, which is surprising given there are regrettable numbers of divorcees who put off finalising financial arrangements in the midst of the stress and upset at the demise of a marriage.

Readers will be helped to give accurate, timely, advice for clients keen to remarry, and those who suspect their former spouse has landed themselves in the 'elephant trap'. Such advice should clearly be communicated in writing.

Remarriage does not always need to be avoided by a client fully aware of its consequences. Some financial remedy provisions are brought to an automatic end by remarriage, for example the receipt of spousal periodical payments. But for the majority of clients who have formally concluded their finances from their previous marriage, and of course obtained a final divorce order (Decree Absolute in old vocabulary), the process is a simple one.

We hope this Guide to Remarriage will alleviate uncertainty, allow confidence, and avoid the elephant trap.

CHAPTER ONE

THE LAW

After a divorce application is issued (divorce 'petition' in the old vocabulary), either spouse to the marriage is entitled to make a claim for financial remedies against the other under the Matrimonial Causes Act 1973 ('MCA').

As the Supreme Court made clear in *Wyatt v Vince* [2015] UKSC 14, there is no time limit for when a financial remedies application must be made, even following a meaningfully long delay. Delay may affect the merits of the claim but not the legal standing to make it.

In *Rossi v Rossi* [2006] EWHC 1482 (Fam), which was acknowledged in *Wyatt v Vince*, Mostyn J was clear that if there is a lengthy delay, a party is entitled to be more confident that a claim will not be brought against them, and they can deal with their assets as they choose. Mostyn J further provided guidance that six years may be considered to be a 'long delay' and so good reason would be required to claim relief after the passing of such time.

It remains good advice that an application for financial remedies should be made promptly unless there is a compelling reason for delay. What constitutes a compelling reason will depend upon the specific circumstances of each case, but the delaying party should be mindful that a long delay could negatively impact upon the claim itself.

Remarriage changes things. Section 28(3) MCA is the key statutory provision, and it has teeth. A spouse who has remarried loses their entitlement to apply for a financial provision order or a property adjustment order in their favour. This can obviously have serious consequences for the remarried party.

Section 28(3) MCA provides as follows:

> 'If after the grant or making of a decree or order dissolving or annulling a marriage either party to that marriage remarries whether at any time before or after the commencement of this Act or forms a civil partnership, that party shall not be entitled to apply, by reference to the grant or making of that decree or order, for a financial provision order in his or her favour, or for a property adjustment order, against the other party to that marriage.'

The parallel provision[1] is set out in Civil Partnership Act 2004, schedule 5, paragraph 48:

> 'If after the making of a dissolution or nullity order one of the civil partners forms a subsequent civil partnership or marriage, that civil partner is not entitled to apply, by reference to the dissolution or nullity order, for:
>
> (a) an order under Part 1 in that civil partner's favour, or
>
> (b) a property adjustment order,
>
> against the other civil partner in the dissolved or annulled civil partnership.'

---

1 When we refer to remarriage this also applies to a subsequent civil partnership.

For the avoidance of doubt, all our references to 'remarriage' include 'subsequent civil partnership'.

The applications caught by the above provisions are those for:

1. Financial provision (section 23 MCA) for periodical payments, secured periodical payments and lump sum provisions; and

2. Property adjustment orders (section 24(1) MCA) for transfer of property, settlement of property, and variation of a nuptial settlement for the benefit of one/both of the parties.

The consequence of remarriage or new civil partnership is that these financial claims cannot be made thereafter – unless an appropriate financial application has already been made by the date of the remarriage ceremony. The types of appropriate financial applications (the prayer within a Form A, divorce petition/application, cross-petition/application and/or answer) are set out in Chapter 3. As further explored below, this does not apply to section 23 MCA claims, regardless of whether an application has been issued prior to the remarriage.

Notably *absent* from the above list are pensions. The bite of the section 28(3) provisions does not apply to pension sharing orders. An application for a pension sharing order *can be made* following the applicant's remarriage. Similarly, remarriage has no effect upon a pension sharing order that has already been made.

Strategically, this can often mean it is sensible, and/or one of your client's only options, to focus on a pension sharing order application if the remarried client is in the 'elephant trap' of having lost their entitlement to apply for financial provision/property adjustment orders. Is there a pension pot that could be the subject of a pension sharing order application when in the elephant trap?

The Welfare Reform and Pensions Act 1999 did not amend section 28(3) MCA to include a pension sharing order as a form of financial relief, so remarriage does not prevent such claim. Many commentators assume this was an oversight and consider that section 28(3) MCA should have been amended on the introduction of pension sharing.

Indeed, there has been loud academic criticism of the exclusion of pension sharing orders from the remarriage trap. The Pension Advisory Group's 2024 report (second edition of their 'A Guide to the Treatment of Pensions on Divorce') rails:

> 'There is no logical reason for pension sharing to be excluded from the remarriage trap. It is believed that the omission of pension sharing by way of amendment from the subsection may result from an oversight on the part of the draftsman.' [161]

Although pension attachment orders are much less commonly made than pension sharing orders (pension attachment orders acknowledged to be 'rare' by the Pensions Advisory Group report of 2019[2]), it is important to clarify that pension attachment orders differ here. A pension attachment order provides payment of a portion of (i) pension income, and/or (ii) a commutable lump sum, and/or (iii) death benefits.

Because pension attachment orders are effectively periodical payments or lump sum orders, they are categorised as financial

---

[2] At page 2 of the Pensions Advisory Group 2019 report 'A Guide to the Treatment of Pensions on Divorce'.

provision orders, and so section 28(3) MCA *does* apply to them. Where a pension attachment order has been made, and the applicant for the pension attachment order then remarries, the order for periodical payments from the pension will cease, albeit the deferred lump sum order will not. Given how rare pension attachment orders have become, it is perhaps an academic point, but a detail to note nonetheless.

The consequence of remarriage upon spousal periodical payments is significant. Whilst cohabitation only becomes a trigger factor for cessation of a periodical payments order if the court order/parties' consent includes it as such, remarriage is starkly different.

Remarriage has an automatic effect: pursuant to section 28(1)(a) MCA spousal periodical payments cannot be ordered to extend beyond the remarriage of the recipient party. Remarriage therefore impacts any existing spousal periodical payments order and a remarried potential recipient's ability to apply for a spousal periodical payments order.

Good timing is key to avoiding the elephant trap. Cautious, sensible wedding planning is rewarded. If the applicant's remarriage is celebrated *after* they have applied for financial remedies against their former spouse, that application may proceed. It may proceed even if the proceedings have not yet been heard, and the only procedural step made at the date of marriage has been issuing.

One of the first questions practitioners need to then ask a remarried client is – whether a valid financial remedies application has been made *before* they have walked down the aisle. As the saying goes – "Marry in haste, repent at leisure".

Meanwhile, the former spouse of the remarried party has no such restrictions. Their right to bring financial claims against their remarried ex remains unencumbered. Assuming of course that they remain unmarried until they issue such a claim.

The case of *E v E* [2008] 1 FLR 220 is the origin of the 'elephant trap' description.[3] Singer J used the term to describe 'a truly cautionary tale' [1]. After their separation, the wife's divorce petition included a claim for all forms of ancillary relief. The husband was the respondent to this divorce petition. The husband had not himself made any application for financial remedies.

Decree Absolute was granted. The former spouses negotiated a financial remedies settlement with the assistance of their solicitors, which resulted in a signed consent order. The drafting had been finalised, but the consent order had not yet been sent to the court to be approved. Presumably without a careful eye on timing and procedure, the husband proceeded to marry his new partner in Bali, at 'a ceremony which, certainly the date if not the place of which, he now no doubt deeply regrets' [1].

Singer J identified 'the brutal outcome' that came about for the husband – he fell into the 'elephant trap of premature remarriage' [14]. Singer J determined: 'the court was never seized, and the court's jurisdiction was never invoked until after the husband had remarried and put it beyond the court's power to contemplate and deal with his application.' [14]. 'I cannot make bricks without any straw, and s.28(3) of the 1973 Act burns the straw. There is no jurisdiction. I refuse the husband's application' [17].

There ensued arguments of legal gymnastics, on which Singer J reached firm, if not potentially harsh, conclusions. He considered

3 Although the *E v E* citation is 2008, the judgment of Singer J is dated 10 October 2006 so it pre-dates the decision of *Whitehouse-Piper v Stokes* [2008] EWCA Civ 1049, heard in July 2008.

that given the only order sought was for the wife to pay the husband a lump sum, she could not apply for such an order against herself even if she was generously minded to do so. 'It would be absurd if you could make an order in favour of a remarried spouse because the other spouse was asking you to, but you could not if that spouse him or herself were asking for the same relief' [13].

These legal gymnastics are one of the reasons the topic of remarriage can become so messy. Debate has continued to rage about 'piggybacking' claims since *E v E* – and this complicated subject is dealt with at Chapter 4 that follows.

Income

A spousal periodical payment claim cannot be pursued by a remarried party. Of course, this does not stop a party who has not remarried seeking periodical payments against their remarried former spouse, if they wish to do so.

Practitioners will be well-familiar with the maintenance 'bar' under section 28(1)(a) MCA under which periodical payments cease following the *recipient*'s remarriage – an automatic trigger factor. N.B. the numbering is not to be confused with a section 28(1A) bar on the extension of a maintenance term.

An oft-asked question by clients in the midst of negotiating/ finalising their finances upon divorce is: 'what happens if I remarry?', or 'what happens if my ex remarries?'. A quick, and/or surprise remarriage of their ex-spouse will make most clients, certainly those in needs cases, feel like the circumstances of their settlement were unfair.

Surely it is for this reason that Form E, paragraph 1.7 asks the author to provide the date of any forthcoming intended marriage, and Form E paragraphs 1.8 and 1.9 ask whether the author is currently living with a new partner or intends to do so within the next six months.

Where a party is cohabiting, intends to cohabit, has remarried, or intends to remarry, Form E paragraph 4.6 requires disclosure of the new partner/spouse's financial circumstances, and the court is entitled to take into account the new partner/spouse's financial circumstances as a resource.

Not for the first time, the public policy reasoning favouring finality in litigation can be at odds with a lay-person's feelings on this subject. It particularly bites in relation to income where maintenance has been capitalised. Clients will no doubt be firmly advised that capitalising maintenance always involves an element of risk-taking for both the payer and payee. The payee risks their needs being more than initially calculated and having to bear an income shortfall alone. Conversely, the payer risks frustration if their ex-spouse flourishes financially beyond what is expected, whether by their personal efforts, or an advantageous remarriage.

Problems with trying to argue remarriage as a *Barder* event (*Barder v Barder (Caluori Intervening)* [1988] AC 20) usually fail at the foreseeability hurdle. In the overwhelming majority of circumstances, even a surprise remarriage will be a possibility, beyond the merely theoretical, at the time of final order or settlement.

The facts of *Dixon v Marchant* [2008] EWCA Civ 11 were stark, and the court's decision surprised many commentators at the time. Mr Dixon paid his wife Mrs Dixon a lump sum to capitalise her joint lives maintenance order. She had firmly denied cohabiting, intending to cohabit, or intending to remarry during the court proceedings and negotiations. Mrs Dixon then remarried, becoming Mrs Marchant, less than seven months after the order was agreed and approved. The question for the court was, per Ward LJ: 'Where a wife remarries shortly after a consent order has provided for payment of a lump sum to capitalize her periodical payments, does that constitute a *Barder*-type event which invalidates the basis or fundamental assumption upon which the order was made?'.

The answer for the majority of the court, in Ward LJ's lead judgment, was no, or at least not necessarily.

The 'man on the Clapham omnibus' might however prefer the view of dissenting Wall LJ, who considered that in these parties' circumstances, Mrs Marchant's remarriage 'makes the order not merely unsustainable, but – on its face – unjust' [34].

The bottom line remains that such situations are intensely fact specific. There are authorities where the need to accommodate the minor children is the dominant feature, and the court has been persuaded that a subsequent financially advantageous remarriage has falsified the fundamental basis of the awards made. Examples here are *Wells v Wells* [1992] 2 FLR 66 and *Williams v Lindley* [2005] EWCA Civ 103.

Despite such examples, there is no blanket principle that can be applied. The court in *Dixon* was careful to note that 'despite the industry of counsel [representing the parties in *Dixon*], neither can produce a case where remarriage as such is the one and only decisive event.' [20]

It is interesting that even in a decision now decades old, *K v K* [2006] 2 FLR 468, Coleridge J was conscious of the tension between the consequences for income claims resulting from cohabitation versus remarriage. The Office for National Statistics tells us that more than 9 in 10 couples who were married in 2021 or 2022 were cohabiting prior to marriage. This is the highest level of cohabitation prior to marriage recorded, and a striking increase over time compared to only 59.6% of couples cohabiting prior to marriage in 1994 (the earliest year that such data is available).

Whilst a recipient's remarriage is an automatic trigger factor for spousal periodical payments under section 28(1)(a) MCA, there remains no such statutory trigger caused by the recipient's cohabitation. It is therefore reliant on the parties in negotiations, or the court in its determination, to proactively include the recipient's cohabitation as a trigger factor for periodical payments ending should they wish to do so. This frequently involves negotiation about the appropriate time-period of cohabitation before the trigger bites.

Perhaps practical reasoning has led policy decision here. It is notoriously awkward and tricky to "prove" cohabitation in the face of a party's denial of living with a partner. Many clients do all they can to avoid needing to resort to such intrusive arguments in the first place.

Nevertheless, back in 2005 (reported in 2006), in his *K v K* judgment, Coleridge J made his views known, at length, on how the law should move on.

> [4] 'Daily, the family courts at all levels and divorce registries around the country are faced by this issue. Is it sufficient to dispose of the issue by saying, as thus far the Court of Appeal has done both in the distant past and more recently (*Fleming v Fleming* [2003] EWCA Civ 1841, [2004] 1 FLR 667), 'it simply depends upon the financial impact of the cohabitation', there is no wider point of principle?'. Is that nowadays a complete and fair

response or as fair as the courts can make it absent reforming legislation? Should payers carry on paying when their former spouses have set up home with another partner and there is nothing but the legal paperwork to distinguish that relationship from the previous marriage? Can cohabiting payees continue to have their cake and eat it by, perhaps cynically, refusing to remarry to avoid the automatic financial consequence of the cessation of an existing periodical payments order?'

[87] 'This is a troubling and messy area of the law and the current legislation enacted against an utterly different social fabric is not adequate to deal with it. The question is how far can the court go to redress the inadequacies of this somewhat superannuated legislation by applying it now in the contemporary context. Obviously, the impact of cohabitation can affect, potentially, both quantum and duration of an ongoing order.'

[88] 'I do not shrink from saying that, in my judgment, nowadays the man on the Clapham omnibus (perhaps more likely now to be found on the crowded underground train) regards it as wholly anomalous and unfair for a cohabiting ex-wife in the circumstances of this wife to continue to receive income provision from a former husband indefinitely, perhaps for the rest of her life or until she chooses to remarry. If cohabitation is to be a social norm surely financial independence from a previous partner, whether married or not must go with it?'

[104] 'Finally, I will leave this part of the case by making two points: (a) I see no reason why nowadays courts

> should not order a termination on 'cohabitation' after a certain period. Section 28(b) of the Matrimonial Causes Act 1973 by no means prohibits it and it would at least provide certainty for the parties. It would, I consider, better reflect modern mores and social behaviour.'

The same approach in *K v K* was not adopted in *Grey v Grey* [2010] 1 FLR 1764, in which the interrelationship of pre and post-marital cohabitation was examined. The dispute stemmed from the illogical position that pre-marital cohabitation should be accounted for, whilst post-marital cohabitation is largely disregarded. In his judgment, Thorpe J summarised his conclusion on the approach in *Fleming v Fleming* as follows:

> 'Thus, in my judgment, the approach indicated by this court in *Fleming v Fleming* remains sound and is sufficiently flexible to enable the court to do justice and to reflect social and moral shifts within our society.' [43]

On that basis, Thorpe J's position was whilst he was 'sympathetic' to Coleridge J's wish in *K v K* 'to move the law on and to achieve greater certainty for practitioners', he recognised 'the power to award financial provision is statutory. There is a limit to the extent to which the courts can interpret statute' [57]. The approach of the court in *Fleming v Fleming* was therefore preferred to that of *K v K*.

Cohabitation can be said to be relevant insofar as reductions are concerned for a payee's considered needs case. If it can be argued that the payee benefits from a secondary income from their cohabiting partner, or there is a benefit to them of reduced living costs, then a reduction could be applied, were the same approach taken as in *Grey v Grey*.

There has been no statutory change since these judgments, whilst the cohabitation statistics have steadily increased.

Maintenance after remarriage

Whilst on the topic of income claims, it raises the following question – does the court retain its power to enforce a maintenance agreement, reached between the parties and finalised via a financial court order, in the event of a party remarrying or forming a new civil partnership?

Firstly, it must be considered whether there a valid maintenance agreement in accordance with section 34 MCA in the event of remarriage. Section 34(1) MCA states the following:

> 'If a maintenance agreement includes a provision purporting to restrict any right to apply to a court for an order containing financial arrangements, then—
>
> (a) that provision shall be void; but
>
> (b) any other financial arrangements contained in the agreement shall not thereby be rendered void or unenforceable and shall, unless they are void or unenforceable for any other reason (and subject to sections 35 and 36 below), be binding on the parties to the agreement'

Section 34(2) MCA sets out what constitutes a maintenance agreement:

> 'any agreement in writing made, whether before or after the commencement of this Act, between the parties to a marriage, being —

(a) an agreement containing financial arrangements, whether made during the continuance or after the dissolution or annulment of the marriage; or

(b) a separation agreement which contains no financial arrangements in a case where no other agreement in writing between the same parties contains such arrangements;

"financial arrangements" means provisions governing the rights and liabilities towards one another when living separately of the parties to a marriage (including a marriage which has been dissolved or annulled) in respect of the making or securing of payments or the disposition or use of any property, including such rights and liabilities with respect to the maintenance or education of any child, whether or not a child of the family.'

The approach is clear, as shown in *T v R (Maintenance after remarriage: agreement)* (Rev 1) [2016] EWFC 26, that even after remarriage, the court retains the power to *enforce* a maintenance agreement.

In *T v R*, the wife had remarried *after* a financial order was made in ancillary relief proceedings by consent. The husband had been paying the wife maintenance (without indexation) for some 16 years including 14 years post her remarriage. An important factual point of this case was that whilst the order provided that the husband pay maintenance until remarriage or further order, as required by the statute, the parties had (by consent) added a recital/preamble that should the wife remarry, the husband will continue maintenance at the rate in force at the time of her remarriage to be index linked (although this could be discharged on capitalisation of the wife's maintenance prior to her remarriage). Following the husband ceasing payments, the wife applied for enforcement. The husband counter applied for variation under section 35 MCA.

Parker J applied the principles of *Wyatt v Vince*, rule 4.4 Family Procedure Rules 2010, and sections 34 and 35 MCA, and concluded that the recited agreement was capable of variation, remarriage not being a bar to the court's power of *variation* here.

Section 35 MCA provides detailed variation/alteration powers for the court:

> '(1) Where a maintenance agreement is for the time being subsisting and each of the parties to the agreement is for the time being either domiciled or resident in England and Wales, then either party may apply to the court for an order under this section.'

N.B. Section 35(4) MCA:

> 'Where the court decides to alter, by order under this section, an agreement by inserting provision for the making or securing by one of the parties to the agreement of periodical payments for the maintenance of the other party or by increasing the rate of the periodical payments which the agreement provides shall be made by one of the parties for the maintenance of the other, the term for which the payments or, as the case may be, the additional payments attributable to the increase are to be made under the agreement as altered by the order shall be such term as the court may specify, subject to the following limits, that is to say —
>
> (a) where the payments will not be secured, the term shall be so defined as not to extend beyond the death

of either of the parties to the agreement or the remarriage of, or formation of a civil partnership by, the party to whom the payments are to be made;

(b) where the payments will be secured, the term shall be so defined as not to extend beyond the death or remarriage of, or formation of a civil partnership by, that party.'

As per the approach in *T v R,* the court retains its powers to *vary a maintenance agreement* in the event of a party's remarriage after a financial order in financial remedy proceedings. It no doubt sits logically that the court retains both its powers of variation and enforcement, as is appropriate.

On that basis, a method to 'escaping' the elephant trap, providing the facts of the case warrant it and there is a financial order for a maintenance agreement already in place prior to a party's remarriage, could be for that party to apply to court for variation and/or enforcement of the maintenance agreement. This could potentially be combined with a pension sharing order application, as addressed below in the capital law section.

Capital

The capital situation for a remarried party can be tricky in practice. A remarrying party would be well placed to understand that, upon their remarriage, they will lose their entitlement to apply for a property adjustment order *if* their financial claims have not been preserved prior to their remarriage.

Section 24(1) MCA captures the court's powers to order a transfer of property, settlement of property, and variation of a nuptial settlement. They are all claims that the remarrying party will lose if they do not preserve them with an appropriate application (as addressed in 'the applications' chapter).

This provision does *not* prevent a party who has *not* remarried from pursuing a claim under section 24(1) MCA against their remarried former spouse, if they choose to do so. The spouse who has not remarried may still bring full capital claims (and indeed, income claims as the payee) if their case warrants it.

It is important to be acutely aware that a remarrying party stands to lose their capital claims if they do not preserve them prior. To lose their legitimate claims prematurely could be financially disastrous for the remarrying party, particularly in circumstances where they may not have anticipated or planned to be financially independent from their former spouse/civil partner. As already stated, the fundamental impact of remarriage on financial claims must indisputably be the reason why the author within paragraph 1.8 of the Form E is required to complete details of their remarriage, and/or their intention to marry within the next six months, together with the requirement of paragraph 4.6 of Form E to set out disclosure of the new partner/spouse's financial circumstances including their capital position. If the remarriage has taken place, then a careful review must be undertaken to understand whether the remarried party can properly pursue capital claims within the proceedings.

The case of *Whitehouse-Piper v Stokes* [2008] EWCA Civ 1049, which is explored in more detail within the 'piggy-back claims' chapter that follows, is a key authority demonstrating the example of the remarriage trap in which the wife had remarried without applying for a financial order. Her reasoning was that the family home, at the time, was in negative equity and so she could not be released from the mortgage. Subsequently, when the family home had increased in value, and after the wife's remarriage, the parties agreed that the wife's legal and beneficial interest in the family home should be transferred to the husband. However, as a result of the wife's remarriage, whilst the court retained the power to transfer the property to the husband as it was beneficial to him, the court considered it did not have the power to order a lump sum payment to benefit the wife. Her remarriage had precluded her from being able to apply for financial remedies in her favour. There is more on this in the piggy-back claims chapter.

Given the capital claims lost by the remarried party in the event that no appropriate application has been made prior (excluding pension sharing orders), it can leave such party in a particularly financially vulnerable situation for the very reason highlighted in *Whitehouse-Piper v Stokes*.

An example which may regularly occur would be where a remarried party continues to jointly own a property in which their former spouse lives with the children, but they left the marriage without formalising an agreement for the living arrangements and/or any future subsequent sale. If the non-resident spouse has remarried, they lose their ability to apply for a transfer or sale of the family home (including a Mesher/Martin order which may otherwise have been appropriate) under the MCA. This could result in the living arrangements continuing indefinitely, without a future sale, as the resident party may choose not to file a financial remedies application if it is not in their interests to do so. In this scenario, and in the absence of any agreement being able to be reached between the parties outside of court proceedings, the remarried, non-resident party would need to pursue alternative claims to move the situation forward.

It is the case therefore that careful consideration must be given as to the timing of any application – in seeking to preserve as many financial claims as possible, as well as how, or if, an appropriate application has been made.

To fail to make an application, or a procedurally correct application in the appropriate form, would be catastrophic to pursuing capital claims. If an application has been appropriately made, then the settlement considerations would be applied of whether any delay was just, and thereafter the case would turn on its own facts.

As explored earlier, a claim for a pension sharing order remains open for a remarried party to pursue regardless of remarriage, effectively because it is an order in its own right. Historically, the Welfare Reform and Pensions Act 1999 did not amend section 28(3) of the MCA to include a pension sharing order as a form of financial relief and so remarriage does not stop a claim for it. A pension attachment order on the other hand is not a 'financial order' within the meaning of section 28(3) MCA as it is considered to be a periodical payments order/and or lump sum order, so the jurisdiction to pursue any such claim following a recipient party's remarriage would end.

A claim for a pension sharing order may well open the ability to pursue pension income on retirement (/aged 55/ maturity of the pension depending on the pension scheme's rules) for the remarried party, but it does not provide maintenance for a potentially significant period of time in-between. The court may further struggle to accept there is a pension need if maintenance was not being paid prior and indeed, the remarried party may be argued to benefit from their new spouse's income and/or pension dependent on the facts in any event. Nonetheless, a pension sharing order at least exists as a procedurally live claim for a remarried party, and can be pursued by a remarried party as successfully as the circumstances of their case merit.

CHAPTER TWO

WHAT ARE THE ALTERNATIVES WHEN IN THE 'ELEPHANT TRAP'?

If an elephant trapped spouse who has remarried has a genuine need for the court's assistance in resolving their circumstances, for example if they still jointly own or have an interest in the family home with their former spouse, then they may need to look to legal alternatives available to them.

So what are the alternatives in the event that capital financial claims have not been preserved prior to remarriage and/or where a maintenance agreement does not already exist with the power of variation or enforcement? As already raised, the remarried party could pursue a claim for a pension sharing order, but their case may not merit such application on its own facts. Perhaps there are no pensions or the low value of the pensions are disproportionate for sharing. Even if there are pensions available for sharing, disputes may arise over the validity of such claims depending on the accrual date of any pensions available to be shared. A solitary pension sharing order claim may not be adequate or realistic, and the heavy limitation on all other capital claims is unlikely to be satisfactory or meet the MCA fairness and equality principles.

If the facts require and justify it, a remarried party can make a claim under the Trusts of Land and Appointment of Trustees Act 1996 ('TOLATA'), an application under section 17 of the Married Women's Property Act 1882, and/or a Schedule 1 Children Act 1989 claim. However, these claims, in contrast to a MCA claim, can only be made in limited circumstances and no doubt will require the court to reflect on whether they are appropriate alternatives, given that practitioners will be aware that the court prefers to be alive to the section 25 MCA factors. Such approaches can cause hesitation and caution from the court in applying or accepting jurisdiction of such alternative procedures for an elephant trapped spouse.

Alternative Dispute Resolution ('*ADR*')

Before embarking on any such alternative applications, ADR should be at least considered and proposed, if not enthusiastically attempted, provided there are no exemptions which apply. As of 29 April 2024, more stringent rules apply, requiring a statement of position (FM5 Form) to be completed no later than 7 days prior to a hearing (most relevant to Schedule 1 claims below), being a more detailed form than the previous FM1 Family Mediation Information and Assessment Form (MIAM), and covering a larger range of ADR options such as:

1. Mediation;

2. Arbitration;

3. Neutral Evaluation; and

4. Collaborative Law.

Under TOLATA, unwillingness to enter into ADR processes without justification may have negative cost consequences, even if the party 'wins' their case; *PGF II SA v OMFS Co 1 Ltd* [2014] 1 WLR 1386. Furthermore, in both TOLATA and Schedule 1 proceedings, the general rule that there is "no order for costs" as in the MCA, does not apply. Orders that one party pays the other's costs are more prevalent in these alternate claims and the inherent risk of a cost consequence should not be forgotten.

Notwithstanding this, the court has made it abundantly clear that Non-Court Dispute Resolution (NCDR) options must be attempted first except in certain circumstances. The FM5 Form now requires more thorough detail addressing what has been attempted, and in the event that no ADR has been attempted, detailed reasons must be given for not having done so. The FM5 Form notes that NCDR does not include a MIAM, the inference being that in the event that mediation is agreed, it should be properly attempted to include at least one joint session, rather than a standalone MIAM. As such, it is crucial that ADR/NCDR is first attempted, where appropriate, in order to meet the court's requirements prior to issuing proceedings and also to reserve the cost claim provision.

Trusts of Land and Appointment of Trustees Act 1996 ('*TOLATA*')

TOLATA as an alternative remedy is only available where there is no jurisdiction under the MCA/CPA (i.e. an MCA application has not been made by either party before the court); *Tee v Tee and Hillman* [1999] 2 FLR 613. A TOLATA application can only focus upon property claims between the parties but it may be a viable alternative for a remarried party in circumstances where they have lost their ability to pursue an application for financial claims under the MCA.

To carefully summarise the approach on TOLATA claims, the first step to understand whether either party has an entitlement to make a claim on the property in question would be to explore whether there is a Declaration of Trust. If there is a Declaration of Trust, this is often strong evidence as to how the proceeds of sale should be divided between the parties. If there is no Declaration of Trust, but there is compelling evidence on how the property was intended to be owned, i.e. there is an express declaration within a Transfer Form or a separate Deed of Trust, it will be binding provided there is no fraud, duress or mistake; *Pankhania v Chandegra* [2012] EWCA Civ 1438.

If the property is solely owned and there is no Declaration of Trust or evidence setting out any beneficial ownership to the contrary, then any claiming party must demonstrate that they have a beneficial interest in the property. This is usually done by way of constructive trust. A constructive trust would require the claiming party to show that there was a common intention (usually proved by an express verbal/written agreement, or potentially via actions and behaviour) that both parties would have an interest in the property, that they acted to their detriment in reliance on that common intention (e.g. contributed towards mortgage repayments, property improvements etc.) and that it would be unconscionable for the other party to deny their interest.

If the property is held in joint names, in the absence of a Declaration of Trust or any formal document setting out ownership, then the starting point and assumption would be that the parties hold the property in equal shares. If one party sought to claim a larger share, they would need to show that there was a common intention to own the property in unequal shares through seeking a declaration of beneficial ownership outside of the presumed equal shares; *Jones v Kernott* [2011] UKSC 53. Such an increased beneficial ownership share could be shown in the same way as above, often being financial contributions towards the upkeep and maintenance of the property.

Whilst a TOLATA claim focuses on property settlement in the absence of any MCA application, there can be a limited income claim, being occupation rent. This is a charge made by a co-owner (the person excluded from a property) against the person living in the property for their exclusive use. On occasions, this can be backdated to the date when the non-resident party vacated the property. However, there is a counterargument, depending on which party was making the monthly repayments and in what share (if there is a mortgage), that the resident party could seek to be compensated for paying the non-resident's share of the monthly mortgage repayments, if that is the case. This is a claim which is more commonly used in cohabitation cases than MCA cases, as in many MCA claims, occupational rent is offset by an alternate contribution whether financially or in the home which generally arise from the section 25 factors. It is yet to be seen whether this is a claim that could be pursed by a payee who lost their income claims by virtue of their remarriage.

A claim under TOLATA can therefore deal with the property, and, at best, some element of income claim. However, where it is governed by the Civil Procedure Rules, its scope is limited owing to its foundation of being evidence based, and therefore losing the fairness and equality principles which provide the MCA its wide powers of redistribution. Where one party's financial contributions and earning capacity may have been limited by virtue of being the homemaker and/or primary child carer, it can result in their non-financial contributions being disregarded on any division of the property in their favour, where they would have otherwise been taken into consideration under the MCA. It is likely that a party would be more motivated to make a TOLATA claim if they needed the property to be disposed of or if they were able to evidence a larger share of ownership.

This approach has been considered in the case of *Miller-Smith v Miller-Smith* [2009] EWCA Civ 1297. At [18], Wilson LJ stated:

> 'I am clear that, confronted with an application under TOLATA between separated spouses, the court should

embark upon the discretionary exercise by asking itself whether the issue raised by the application can reasonably be left to be resolved within an application for ancillary relief following divorce.

It is in principle much more desirable that an issue, as here, about sale of the home should be resolved within an application for ancillary relief. For there the court will undertake a holistic examination of all aspects of the parties' finances, needs, contributions etc; will devise the fairest set of arrangements for the future housing and finances of each of them; and, to that end, will provide for the transfer of capital, as well perhaps as for payment of future income, from one to the other.

By an order under TOLATA, on the other hand, the court lays down only one piece of the jigsaw, namely that the home be sold, without its being able to survey the whole picture by laying down the others. So at this threshold stage of the enquiry into an application under TOLATA between spouses the court will, in particular, have regard to the question whether, within a time-frame tolerable in all the circumstances, the parties will become able to apply for ancillary relief.

Furthermore if, at first sight, there appears to the court to be any measurable chance that, on an application for ancillary relief made within that time-frame, the respondent to the application for an order for sale under TOLATA will be able to preserve her or his occupation of the home by securing an outright transfer of ownership of it or a variation of the trust, it is hard to conceive that an order for sale would reflect a proper exercise of discretion.'

A respondent who is barred by section 28(3) MCA in bringing financial claims as a result of their remarriage could consider issuing TOLATA proceedings to be consolidated with the applicant/petitioner's application for financial remedy proceedings in divorce proceedings. It is likely these would be rare factual circumstances and such an approach should be approached with caution given the court's disapproval in *Tee v Tee and Hillman* [1999] 2 FLR 613 of the parties engaging in TOLATA proceedings where it would have only been restricted to proprietary law, losing the ability to apply the section 25 MCA checklist, being fundamental in matrimonial cases. It is anticipated that the court would remain cautious in losing its jurisdiction over the principles of fairness and equality.

Married Women's Property Act 1882 ('*MWPA*')

Further including: CPA / Part IV Family Law Act 1996 ('FLA') / Matrimonial Proceedings and Property Act 1970 ('MPPA') / Matrimonial Causes (Property and Maintenance) Act 1958 ('MCPMA') / Law Reform (Miscellaneous Provisions) Act 1970 ('LRA').

Leading with the MWPA, this is a rarely used statue which was originally enacted primarily to allow married women to own and control property, income, and deal with inheritance in their own right. It further granted women equal inheritance rights over property of intestate children, and it made both parents liable to maintain their children if they held separate property. Historically, this was a turning-point statute for women's rights.

The MWPA is further extended by the Law of Property Act 1922 which granted spouses (at the time, a husband and wife) the ability to inherit each other's property, and also granted them equal inheritance rights over property of intestate children.

The most common application under MWPA is a Section 17 claim for married parties, the equivalent provision being contained in Section 66 of the CPA. For ease of this section, we refer to this as a Section 17 claim. This is mirrored by the following alternatives, providing a broader scope of applicants:

1. Part IV FLA 1996 – Available to all parties who are associated persons (as defined in section 62 FLA).

2. Section 39 MPPA 1970 (section 68, CPA) – Available to parties who were formerly married or in a civil partnership, but the section 17 claim must be made within 3 years following annulment, divorce or dissolution.

3. Section 7 MCPMA (Section 67, CPA) – Available to parties who are still married or in a civil partnership.

4. Section 2 LRA – Available to parties who have terminated their engagement to marry.

A Section 17 claim could therefore be pursued as follows:

1. As an alternative to TOLATA, to determine the issue of ownership of property without seeking a divorce or dissolution; and/or

2. To pursue orders that the court may not ordinarily make under TOLATA, such as an interim order for sale, interim use of chattels and choses in action; and/or

3. To pursue wider powers, to include lump sum payment orders representative of the assessed value of the other party's

beneficial interest in the property (or otherwise, a 'buy out' transfer); and/or

4. As an alternative available to parties who did not have a legally recognised marriage, *those who have already completed their divorce or dissolution* (providing it is made within 3 years of granting) or parties who cannot bring a claim under the MCA.

A section 17 claim can be made using the Part 18 procedure within existing financial remedy proceedings where it gives the court the appropriate jurisdiction to direct interim orders for sale and interim use of chattels (in line with point 2 above).

The wide scope of providing the court with the discretion to make 'such order with respect to the property as it thinks fit' may grant powers which reach a wider scope of applications and orders to be made outside of the limitations of TOLATA. It is also possible for this application to be joined with Schedule 1 applications (addressed below). As such, it may be a "safer" application if there are low prospects of success with a TOLATA application and where the general rule that costs follow does not apply (given that the Family Procedure Rules 28.3 do not apply).

This is not a failsafe however as there may still be limitations where the court does not have jurisdiction to make orders beyond the scope of the MCA. In line with the approach in *Tee v Tee and Hillman* [1999] 2 FLR 613, the court may still be reluctant to lose its powers to apply the fairness principles if there is any potential of consolidating proceedings with any live MCA proceedings.

Interestingly, in a footnote to paragraph [8] of *SR v. HR, SC* [2018] EWHC 606 (Fam), there is a discussion between Mostyn J and Cobb J in which they discuss whether the MCA provides the power to make an interim order for sale and suggests that if not, an application under section 17 MWPA could be used to make such order. This does not appear to have been tried and tested yet, but it may be an indicator that applying this approach to remarriage is not completely out of reach.

Schedule 1, Children Act 1989

Another alternate option that could be explored is a Schedule 1 Children Act claim for financial provision for the benefit of a child. However, there are limited circumstances where this will be a relevant alternative option in circumstances where either party has remarried. This claim is generally used by unmarried parties but could well apply in cases where neither party has made an MCA application.

Where relevant, Schedule 1 proceedings may be a way of ensuring fairness principles are accounted for in the event that one party is left only with TOLATA proceedings being realistically available. A claim under Schedule 1 could seek for the court to consider the housing needs for the benefit of the child thus, the court has the power to make a wider scope of orders dealing with properties i.e. sale, transfer or deferred sale, with the trigger event likely being the end of the youngest child's minority or finishing their education (thereby often only delaying the inevitable). It is not unusual for Schedule 1 proceedings and TOLATA proceedings to be consolidated or run alongside one another subject to whichever proceedings may secure a better outcome for each applying party.

If the remarried party also seeks additional maintenance-based provision for the child/children of the family, then they are likely to rely on the Child Maintenance Service ('CMS'). The CMS has jurisdiction over cases where the payer (parent with whom the children spend less time overnight) earns less than £156,000 gross per annum (and so under the 'maximum assessment'). In circumstances where the payer earns above the 'maximum assessment', additional claims can also be run under Schedule 1 as follows:

1. Top up orders for maintenance;
2. Lump sums;
3. Payment of school fees;
4. Carer's allowance i.e. childcare costs, nanny etc.; and/or
5. Purchasing/transferring a property to the other party effectively on trust to be returned on the child's majority or finishing of education.

In cases where there is a child with disabilities, under Section 8 Child Support Act 1991 ('CSA') the court retains its power to make a maintenance order on behalf of a child in receipt of a disability living allowance (DLA) and/or Personal Independent Payment (PIP) and thus, the court can make a maintenance order providing it is made 'to meet some or all of any expenses attributable to the child's disability'; Section 8(8) CSA.

This may be a further mechanism available to grant powers to the court outside of dealing only with property matters, which generally restrict TOLATA applications. There may even be scope to consolidate this with a section 17 claim but, as before, this does not appear to have been attempted yet.

A Schedule 1 application requires full financial disclosure from both parties, and the size of the award would take into account the non-resident parent's resources (unless the 'millionaire's defence' can be applied), including the non-resident parent's standard of living. Such an award will require the court to consider 'all the circumstances of the case' including Schedule 1(4)(1):

a) the income, earning capacity, property and other financial resources which each person mentioned in sub-paragraph (4) has or is likely to have in the foreseeable future;

b) the financial needs, obligations and responsibilities which each person mentioned in sub-paragraph (4) has or is likely to have in the foreseeable future;

c) the financial needs of the child;

d) the income, earning capacity (if any), property and other financial resources of the child;

e) any physical or mental disability of the child; and

f) the manner in which the child was being, or was expected to be, educated or trained.

A Schedule 1 application, where relevant, can therefore be more wide-reaching than an application under TOLATA, and take into account many mirroring principles of the MCA, often favouring the primary carer of the children if they are less financially secure than the party against whom they are claiming. However, such a claim is usually limited to the minority of the children and/or completion of their education. A Schedule 1 application may therefore fail to secure long-term financial provision for the more financially vulnerable party beyond their children reaching majority age, therefore not providing for them in the same way that the longevity of the MCA might otherwise have done.

CHAPTER THREE

THE APPLICATION

Remarriage clearly obstructs financial applications for a remarrying spouse. However, some claims can be preserved in situations where a financial remedies application is issued prior to that spouse's remarriage, even if other claims are terminated and therefore cannot be pursued following remarriage (e.g. the receiving party's income/maintenance claims). That is not to ignore that financial claims can be preserved in some circumstances within a divorce application itself.

It is consequently important to consider what a valid application is for financial remedies and whether, and when, those claims can be preserved prior to remarriage.

An application for financial remedies can be made in two ways:

1. Form A: Financial remedies application; and/or

2. Form D8: Application for a divorce in Form D8 (divorce petition in old language).

It is further possible, in limited and untested circumstances, that an application could be argued to have been made via Form D8B as a response to a divorce application/petition by the respondent, detailed below.

Notwithstanding the various application types, the significant issue of the timing of bringing a claim is critically important, as previously examined in 'The Law' chapter. Procedurally, the longer there is a delay, the higher the risk is of the court requiring good reason for delay, particularly over the six-year mark, thereby impacting on the merit of pursuing financial claims. Furthermore, with delay, the practical reality is that documents become lost or unavailable, parties' recollections and memories become more opaque and less reliable, and so there is a higher risk of the court reaching an unjust decision.

Form A[4]

Readers will be aware that the Form A application triggers financial remedy proceedings. When preparing a Form A application for financial remedies, it prompts a 'menu' setting out a prescriptive breakdown of which financial orders are being applied for. It must be confirmed on the form whether the financial claim applications sit as fresh applications, or whether they stem from the financial application and permission confirmed within the divorce prayer. This therefore very clearly preserves the remarrying party's ability to bring claims, providing this application is submitted prior their remarriage. The financial claims within the Form A can be seen here:

4 https://assets.publishing.service.gov.uk/media/6628e39db0ace32985a7e5a5/Form_A_0424.pdf

tick the statement that applies	and	tick one or more of the following orders
The applicant intends: ☐ **to apply** to the Court for *or* ☐ **to proceed with** the application in the ☐ divorce ☐ dissolution ☐ nullity ☐ annulment ☐ (judicial) separation application for *or* ☐ **to apply to vary**		☐ an order for maintenance pending suit/outcome of proceedings ☐ a lump sum order ☐ a property adjustment order ☐ a settlement or a transfer of property for the benefit of the child(ren) ☐ a periodical payments order **together with** other financial provision ☐ a pension sharing order ☐ a pension compensation sharing order
☐ **to apply to discharge** a periodical payments order **and** to substitute for it one or more orders opposite		☐ a lump sum order ☐ a property adjustment order ☐ a pension sharing order ☐ a pension compensation sharing order

Additional information required

Are you applying for an order by consent in terms of written agreement (a consent order)?	☐ **Yes, attach the draft order to this form** ☐ No

A financial remedies application via Form A is widely accepted as the standard and safest mechanism of triggering financial claims for the applicant. As used to be the procedure historically, Forms A were so commonly accepted in generating financial claims that when parties reached financial settlement by consent, a respondent to a consent order application would file their own Form A application 'for dismissal purposes', giving the court the power to dismiss their financial claims alongside the applicant's following approval and sealing of any such order.

Acceptance of issuing financial remedies and their preservation of claims in the event of remarriage can be said to stem back to the case of *Nixon v Fox* [1978] 3 All ER 995 where the wife had filed her notice of application for ancillary relief (application for financial remedy proceedings), ticking that she was applying for periodical payments and secured periodical payments for the benefit for the children. The wife remarried following her application, resulting in a section 28(3) MCA bar. The wife attempted to apply to extend her application post-remarriage, to include a claim for a lump sum and transfer of property order for her benefit. However, the court did not uphold her application as she had not protected herself by ticking those boxes in her original application and had lost the power to make such claims retrospectively following her remarriage. Had the wife ticked the correct boxes of those additional claims she sought, and not just the maintenance claims, it is likely that she would have preserved her capital claims regardless of her remarriage (although the merit of any such application would ride on the facts of the case).

Form D8[5] – Applicant and cross-applying respondent

Readers will be further aware that Form D8 is the application to start divorce proceedings. Within the Form D8 (whether the paper or online version), financial claims can be also protected at the outset in the event of remarriage prior to bringing financial remedy proceedings.

The previous divorce petition and the new divorce application form contain a 'prayer' which sets out whether the applicant(s) want to apply for a financial order for themselves and/or the children. It is possible in a joint divorce application for both applicants to tick 'yes' separately indicating their own separate wish to apply for a financial order. If the applicant(s) ticked 'yes', then they preserve their ability to pursue financial claims.

Notably within the current divorce application, the court has issued a warning in the notes section at question 8.1 that if either party ticks 'no' and subsequently remarries or forms another civil partnership, they can no longer apply for financial relief. See here:

5 https://assets.publishing.service.gov.uk/media/66190bbbc1d297c6ad1dfe39/D8_0324.pdf

8.1 Do you want to apply for a financial order?

Sole applicant or applicant 1

Yes, I want to apply for a financial order for (select all that apply)

myself

the children

No

Applicant 2

Yes, I want to apply for a financial order for (select all that apply)

myself

the children

No

uk/money-property-when-relationship-ends/apply-for-a-financial-order

If you answer 'No' to question 8.1 you can still apply for a financial order in the future, but only **until you remarry or form** another **civil partnership**. This restriction does not apply to pension sharing or pension compensation sharing orders.

If you are unsure what to do here it is recommended you seek legal advice.

Please note that decisions regarding child maintenance are usually made by agreement or by the Child Maintenance Service and the court can only make these orders under certain circumstances.

The sole applicant or the joint applicants apply for the following:

9.1 The application

That the

- marriage be dissolved
- civil partnership be dissolved

The sole applicant or applicant 1 wishes to apply for the following

9.2 Financial Order (if you ticked 'Yes' to the question at 8.1 and wish to make an application for a Financial Order)

That a financial order may be granted for:

- The sole applicant or applicant 1
- For the children

Applicant 2 wishes to apply for the following

9.3 Financial Order (if you ticked 'Yes' to the question at 8.1 and wish to make an application for a Financial Order)

That a financial order may be granted for:

- Applicant 2
- For the children

The same protection of financial claims applies in the event that the remarrying party is a respondent to the first divorce application/ petition, but they choose to issue their own cross application, ticking 'yes' to confirm their intention to apply for a financial order.

In the event therefore, that the applying party has remarried but had ticked in the divorce application to indicate that they will proceed with their application for financial claims, that party can proceed with their financial claims application after remarriage. As such, there is no jurisdictional bar to an application for financial claims remaining available, if it has been correctly secured within the divorce application. Notwithstanding this, the facts of that party's remarriage and case would, of course be relevant on the merits as to the appropriate outcome.

This is somewhat supported by the case of *Wilson v Wilson* [1975] 3 All ER 464, in which the remarried wife had applied for maintenance pending suit and permanent spousal periodical payments in her prayer within her divorce petition. The wife had however, failed to tick that she was pursuing a claim for a lump sum, which she later sought after her remarriage. As a result, the court could not allow her to vary her application post-remarriage and her application failed. It is raised that this case is only somewhat supportive of the current approach as it is important to remember that this case is historic and relevant during the 'old' divorce process. At the time when this case was being heard, divorce prayers set out which financial claims were being pursued prescriptively, in a similar way to which the Form A does now. It seems safe to assume that if the wife had included an application for a lump sum within her divorce petition prayer, that she would have secured her claim regardless of her remarriage. As such, the same assumption can be drawn that if the overarching financial prayer box were to be ticked now, that such financial claims would be preserved in the event of remarriage.

It is however clearly the case that the application for divorce has had many revisions over the years – the most recent simplifying a financial claim as a coverall, rather than the breakdown menu of financial claims as they used to be. In advising clients who have already made historic applications, practitioners must be careful to ensure that they have sight of the sealed divorce petition(s), particularly in older divorces, to understand what, if any, financial claims have been applied for. That being said, if an applicant is considering opening their financial claims post-remarriage, with divorce proceedings of that age they are likely to be faced with issue of their delay undermining the merits of any such application.

Form D8 – Respondent

Importantly, looking at the previous divorce process, the respondent's acknowledgment of service in response to a divorce petition alone does not go far enough to preserve their own financial claims. In *Hargood (formerly Jenkins) v Jenkins* [1978] Fam 148, a 'mere answer given in an acknowledgment of service' to a divorce petition, indicating an intention to apply for a financial order, was not enough to be considered to be an application, and it could not therefore avoid the section 28(3) MCA bar following the wife's remarriage.

It must therefore be assumed that an acknowledgment of service within the old divorce process, and therefore likely also the current response form, would not be enough to protect the respondent's financial claims. If that was the respondent's intention, they would need to either cross-apply in divorce (although the merits of doing so may be limited under the new law and process) and/or apply for financial remedy proceedings.

Conversely, the Form D8B[6], being the answer form for a respondent to a divorce or dissolution application, does not contain a specific opportunity for the respondent to tick boxes indicating their intention to apply for a financial order, however there is a general orders box at Part 4:

6 https://assets.publishing.service.gov.uk/media/65f9676ca4d4f3001 10352d4/D8B_0324.pdf

Part 4 Orders requested

☐ For the reasons above I ask the court to dismiss the Petitioner's/Applicant's petition/application

☐ Other

If Other, please specify any other order requested, apart from a costs order (see Part 5).

It is possible that a respondent *could* tick 'other' and complete the box under 'orders requested' to set out their intention to apply for a financial order. This would be a 'back door' approach and has not yet been tested. In light of the strict approach in *Hargood (formerly Jenkins) v Jenkins*, it should be approached cautiously.

Approach

As already stated above, the safest way to preserve financial claims is with an appropriately completed Form A. However, all is not lost if remarriage has taken place prior to having done so. If the applicant has applied for financial orders within their divorce petition/application and/or the respondent has done so by way of a cross-application for divorce, then they have likely preserved their financial claims in the event of their early remarriage.

Timing is crucial. The first consideration must be whether the remarrying party is the applicant or respondent in divorce proceedings. If the remarrying party is the applicant in divorce and their remarriage has taken place before Form A application, but they ticked the financial claims box on their divorce petition/application, they can proceed with a Form A application at any time they see fit including *after* their remarriage.

If the remarrying party is the respondent in divorce proceedings (and/or is the applicant in the divorce but failed to tick the financial claims box), and they did not make a counterapplication in divorce ticking the financial claims box, then they would need to issue a Form A application *before* their remarriage.

Given that the strongest and known approach to preserve as many financial claims as possible is an application via Form A, it would no doubt be sensible for that application to be issued promptly to instigate proceedings prior to the party's remarriage to preserve as many financial claims as possible.

In acting cautiously, a two-pronged approach may be safer rather than relying on a divorce application alone, based on historic case law. Even though a prayer completed within the divorce application/petition, cross application/petition and/or answer can be regarded as an application to preserve financial claims of a capital nature without requiring a separate application in Form A to have also been issued, it is clearly good practice to also file a Form A application prior to that party remarrying or entering into a new civil partnership. In the event that remarriage has already happened, an application for a pension sharing order (the court's retention of such powers having been dealt with above), could still be made depending on the circumstances of the case.

Any remarrying party must therefore give careful consideration as to whether to promptly issue a Form A application in their divorce prior to their remarriage. It would be prudent to advise a client promptly and in writing, once made aware of their intention to remarry or enter into a civil partnership before their current divorce proceedings have been concluded, that they should issue an application via Form A prior to their remarriage or new civil partnership. As dealt with in the earlier chapters, this would safely preserve their financial claims of a capital nature albeit of course their case would then be considered based on its own facts and merits.

CHAPTER FOUR

PIGGY-BACK CLAIMS

Returning to statute is usually the lawyer's preferred starting point to make sense of complicated law. Section 28(3) MCA provides admirable clarity. Yet there remains debate on the issue known as 'piggy-back claims'.

Section 28(3) is repeated again here for ease. For the elephant-trapped spouse, 'that party shall not be entitled to apply… for a financial provision order in his or her favour, or for a property adjustment order, against the other party to that marriage.'

So far, so clear, that the elephant-trapped spouse cannot make such an application.

But what if the application is made by the other ex-spouse? What if the court is already seized with a financial remedies application, legitimately made, by the other spouse? Is remarriage of spouse two a bar to provision being made in their favour whilst proceedings are being determined for spouse one? Can the remarried spouse piggy-back their claims on their former spouse's application?

Forty years of jurisprudence has yet to resolve the debate on this issue. And it is still raging.

Thorpe LJ in *Whitehouse-Piper v Stokes* [2008] EWCA Civ 1049 considered the matter to have been resolved by *Robin v Robin* [1983] 4 FLR 632 – that a remarried spouse cannot rely on their ex-spouse making an application on which to piggy-back their claims. Per Thorpe LJ in *Whitehouse-Piper*:

> 'The case of *Robin v Robin* is now antique, and any decision on the application of section 28(3) can only be drawn from the judgment of Dunn LJ, who at that point spoke obiter.
>
> However, in his obiter dictum he was very plain that if the court's jurisdiction rests solely on an application by one spouse, the other spouse cannot as it were find his jurisdictional base within that application. A respondent to a divorce petition had to issue some application, either by way of prayer within an answer or by issue of application thereafter, in order to found jurisdiction.
>
> The judge surmounted the difficulty which he had himself observed by reference to a much later decision of this court in *Tee v Tee and Hillman* [1999] 2 FLR 613, where the court had particularly disapproved of parties engaging in TOLATA proceedings when their fundamental dispute related to a property and nothing else but a property where the court in doing justice was not restricted to proprietary law but could have regard to all the circumstances imported by the court's section 25 jurisdiction. And that is how the judge overcame the jurisdictional problem.'

However, despite such clear dicta, the outcome on the facts of that case perhaps points in a different direction. In *Whitehouse-Piper* neither (i) the first instance District Judge, (ii) the Circuit Judge on appeal, nor (iii) the Court of Appeal on second appeal, considered there existed any jurisdictional obstacle to a property adjustment order being made in favour of the remarried husband. Despite it being only the wife's (jurisdictionally sound) Form A that was before the court to found such an application.

Perhaps too much case law gloss has been applied to the statute wording. Section 28(3) bars entitlement to *make* an application: 'shall not be entitled to apply'. This is narrower wording than, for example, that used in section 28(1)(a) regarding periodical payments. For the latter, the prohibition is broader – the term of the order is simply not jurisdictionally permitted to extend beyond the remarriage of the payee: 'the term… shall be so defined as not to extend beyond… the remarriage'.

This semantic difference may be fertile ground for argument in the right 'test case' in future. The statute wording at section 28(3), unlike section 28(1)(a) above, does not seem to explicitly impede the court making financial provision or property adjustment orders in the remarried spouse's favour.

The wording of section 23 and section 24 MCA (financial provision orders and property adjustment orders) also bears re-reading. Those sections refer to the court's powers to order financial provision to be made by one party in favour of 'the other' (party).

Does there need to be a revised semantic examination of the statute? The combined effect of contrasting these other MCA provisions could mean that the statutory prohibition at section 28(3) is in fact limited to the *making* of an application – and piggy-backing is permissible.

We remain in the dark about how successfully this argument could be run, and how the higher courts would determine the piggy-backing debate. The judgment of Mostyn J in *CB v EB* [2020] EWFC 72 teased the issue – Mostyn J referring to a similar issue as a 'problematic question', but he concluded it was one he did not need to resolve in that case [70].

Mostyn J hinted that piggy-backing was not something he would deem permissible, as he commented he was 'not convinced' by the argument that 'the bar on the [remarried] husband issuing an application does not prevent the court from varying the orders in his favour' [68]. But he did recognise that the topic remains unresolved, stating that if the matter (on the facts of that case) needed determination by a higher court in the future, then the question of whether the remarried husband was statutorily barred from having his application determined would have 'to be looked at very carefully' [70].

Through his (joint) chairmanship of the Financial Remedies Working Group in 2014, Mostyn J had already attempted to bypass this debate and resolve uncertainty. It was a recommendation of the 2014 Financial Remedies Working Group (chaired by Mostyn J and Cobb J) that Form A should be amended, so as soon as one party to the marriage issues Form A, all possible financial order applications by both spouses should be deemed to have been made, and may be granted or dismissed by the court without the need for further application.[7] If this recommendation had been enacted, or is enacted in the future, there would be no need for piggy-backing arguments. However, over a decade later there is still no such procedural change.

Although an Isle of Man decision, the appeal case of *Hyslop v Hyslop* 2DS 2022/13 & 2DS 2023/03 includes detailed analysis of the remarriage authorities and draws some interesting conclusions. Whilst not a UK decision, the appeal tribunal included Michael Horton KC sitting as an Acting Deemster.

7 Final report of the Financial Remedies Working Group, 15 December 2014, page 2.

Shortly after separation, Mrs Hyslop initiated divorce proceedings. Decree Nisi was granted in January 2015. In September 2015 she applied for financial provision. In November 2017, before the anticipated date listed for their final hearing, the parties reached Heads of Agreement. A financial remedies consent order was approved by the court in December 2017. Mr Hyslop remarried a year later in December 2018.

Mr and Mrs Hyslop had agreed a pension sharing order in respect of the wife's RBS pension as part of their settlement. However, for reasons unknown to the parties at the time, the pension sharing order was 'impossible to enforce' [20], due to geographical/jurisdictional constraints on the pension fund managers implementing a pension sharing order made by an Isle of Man court regarding a pension held in England in Wales. The pension managers said they were only able to act on orders made by a UK court. This Isle of Man pension law loophole frustratingly made it impossible to enforce a pension sharing order made in the Isle of Man against pension assets held in England, and vice versa [20].

The husband, the intended beneficiary of the pension sharing order, had subsequently remarried. Once the problem with the pension sharing order came to light, the husband made an application, under the 'liberty to apply' provision in his 2017 final order for the court's assistance with the implementation of the pension sharing order already made.

The wife took a fairly hostile, albeit strategic, position – arguing that it was the husband's responsibility, as the potential beneficiary of the pension share, to have ensured that procedurally the pension sharing order was sound, and it was his fault for not having understood the mistake. She further argued that the husband's remarriage prevented him from applying for further financial provision. The relevant Isle of Man statute is the Matrimonial Proceedings Act 2003, where the section 28(3) MCA wording is exactly mirrored in section 40(4) as follows:

> 'If, after the making of a divorce order or annulment order, either party to that marriage remarries (whether at any time before or after the commencement of this Act), that party shall not be entitled to apply, by reference to the making of that order, for a financial provision order in his or her favour, or for a property adjustment order, against the other party to that marriage.'

The question for the court was what could or should have been done 'about the impossibility of implementing' that pension sharing order [1]. Could there be a capital provision in favour of the remarried husband, as a substitute for the value he was denied under the ineffective pension sharing order? Or was the court 'prevented from making such capital provision by Mr Hyslop's remarriage.' [2]

The pension sharing order exemption under section 28(3) MCA was obviously of no use to Mr Hyslop. He was prevented by his remarriage from making an application for financial provision, save for seeking a pension sharing order, but do to so would be purposeless as the only pension asset was the RBS pension that had caused the implementation difficulties.

Hyslop immediately focused on the point in *Whitehouse-Piper*: 'what this case [*Whitehouse-Piper*] does show is that even where the [remarried] husband, the net recipient of capital under the order, had not made an application, it was open to the court on the wife's application to make an order in his favour, provided that that had been made clear as part of the proceedings' [172].

The court in *Hyslop* was interested in the legitimacy of piggy-backing claims. 'While Dunn LJ [in *Robin v Robin*] expressed himself in strong terms that the court could not make an order for ancillary relief in favour of A unless A had made an application for such an order, Eveleigh LJ refrained from deciding the case on that basis. As such, in our judgment, the ratio of *Robin* says nothing about the remarriage trap.' [156].

The Isle of Man court considered it a step too far to suggest that 'once one party makes an application for ancillary relief, all matters were before the court.' [182]. At [181] the court concluded:

> '(1) although it was suggested in *Robin v Robin* that it is not open to make, for instance, a property adjustment order in favour of a party who has not themselves made an application for it, in our view that is wrong. It is open for Party A to apply for orders against themselves. On such an application, an order could therefore be made in favour of Party B.
>
> (2) where no application is made by Party A for orders against himself or herself, and Party B has remarried before making any application, and Party A has all the assets, the court cannot make any order in favour of Party B: *E v E.*
>
> ...
>
> (5) given that lump sum provision and property adjustment provision is seen as equivalent, we consider that a court is not precluded from making one or other order in favour of a person who is caught by the remarriage trap provided that such a person is not the net recipient of capital under the overall order. For instance, take a straightforward case where the only significant asset is the matrimonial home held in joint names. The

> wife applies for financial provision and the husband makes no such application, and then subsequently remarries before the wife's application is determined. On her application, the wife seeks an outright transfer of the home into her sole name. The husband's response is to accept a transfer from the wife from the joint names of the parties into the wife's sole name, but with a charge back on Mesher terms, deferring the sale or realisation of the husband's interest until the children had grown up. There is no reason why the court could not make that order even though the husband was caught by the remarriage trap, provided that the husband's deferred interest did not exceed 50% (i.e. he was not the net recipient of ancillary relief). Such an order could be done in a number of ways, but could include effectively a lump sum order in favour of the husband with a deferred entitlement to the lump sum, and the wife undertaking to provide security for the payment of that lump sum as a condition of the transfer to her of the former matrimonial home. Such an order is perfectly permissible notwithstanding his remarriage.'

The Isle of Man court's views in *Hyslop* on piggy-backing are emphatic, and add fuel to the debate that continues in this jurisdiction. The concept of a net capital gain needing to be calculated is a novel approach to the elephant trap problem. It remains to be seen whether the courts in England and Wales would similarly conclude that piggy-backing can be legitimate without statutory change.

MS v FS (No. 3) [2023] EWFC 245 is a case from this jurisdiction that has been decided since *Hyslop*. It was heard by DDJ Mehta at the Central Family Court, no doubt reported in part due to the interesting remarriage arguments.

The wife's position in *MS v FS* was that because the husband had remarried and he had not applied for financial remedy proceedings via Form A in time, the husband was barred by section 28(3) MCA, instead leaving the husband only with the power to pursue claims under TOLATA. The wife's Form A was the only financial application before the court. Both husband and wife had since remarried, but the wife had done so years after making her Form A application.

She strongly argued the more orthodox position that the husband could not piggy-back off her claims in the absence of him having made his own application, in reliance on *Robin v Robin* [1983] 4 FLR 632 and *E v E* [2008] 1 FLR 221. The husband's counter argument was that the wife was in fact the party applying for a property adjustment order in her favour, and the court ought to consider the wife's application.

The facts of *MS v FS* are hopefully beyond the ordinary parameters of most parties' behaviour. Recorder Allen KC previously heard applications from the husband to set aside the final financial consent order that had been approved by the court in 2011, after the parties had separated in 2009/2010. Recorder Allen KC made findings that the husband had been unaware of both the divorce and financial remedy proceedings at that time, and had not signed the Acknowledgment of Service, Form D81, consent order, nor TR1 that followed. These documents had been fraudulently signed by the wife, or someone acting on her behalf. The final financial consent order previously approved by the court must therefore be set aside. The wife was ordered to pay 80% of the husband's costs on the indemnity basis.

These facts do muddy the waters of the piggy-backing arguments. DDJ Mehta concluded: 'It is now impossible to know' whether the husband would have filed a Form A before he remarried in 2018, as 'he was deprived of that opportunity by wife's fraudulent acts' [30]. As a matter of simple fact however, no Form A was filed by husband, which allowed the wife to run the purist argument that, relying on *E v E*, the husband could not rely on the wife's application to seek an order for financial provision after his remarriage.

The court considered the Court of Appeal authority of *Whitehouse-Piper v Stokes* [2008] EWCA Civ 1049, discussed above, which refers to the case of *Robin v Robin* (1983) 4 FLR 632 as *'antique'* [32]. Lord Justice Thorpe stated there:

> 'Accordingly, it seems to me plain that the short answer to this appeal is that the wife applied, by her petition, for all forms of ancillary relief. That entitled her to issue a notice of intention to proceed in Form A despite the fact that the application be filed with the court after remarriage. She took that step on 2 November. She sought an order against herself which was duly achieved. All she failed to do was to show any discretionary entitlement to a balancing lump sum. The capacity for a party to seek a transfer order against him or herself is clearly established by the decision of this court in Dart v Dart [1996] 2 FLR 286. Accordingly the jurisdictional point, quite keenly perceived by HHJ Mitchell, does not directly arise in this case. The answer to the problem that he perceived is to be found clearly in the procedure. I do not consider that it is necessary to engage, as the judge did, in an analysis of previous decisions of this court.' [32]

DDJ Mehta's analysis of *Whitehouse-Piper v Stokes* was as follows:

> 'In that authority, it is clear, that a party has the capacity to seek a transfer of property order against themselves. In

> support of that proposition, is the fact that the Court makes such orders all the time. The Court often finds itself making orders that transfer assets away from the applicant, or indeed making orders against their income in favour of the respondent' [33].

Unsurprisingly, there were factual considerations relevant to *MS v FS* that hopefully would not be present in most cases – fraudulent behaviour. The principle that 'parties should not be allowed to benefit from their own fraudulent acts' [35] of course played a part in DDJ Mehta's decision making. The court agreed that 'wife should be treated as applying for a property adjustment order in respect of the family home, which was in joint names, as that would be the position absent her fraud' [36].

The court 'dismiss[ed] wife's legal argument that the husband is debarred from pursuing his application in these proceedings' [38]. The wife was ordered to pay the husband a lump sum, on the basis that she would remain living in the former family home, and the husband's interest as joint beneficial and legal owner of the property would then be discharged. There would be a default order for sale if the wife failed to pay the lump sum by the deadline imposed.

MS v FS sets the scene well for further interesting remarriage arguments in litigation. The decision was however not able to provide the clear answers on piggybacking that can only be reached by a higher court authority or statutory change.

CHAPTER FIVE

COMPETING CLAIMS

This is a topic that can often need to be considered alongside that of remarriage. It is raised briefly here in case of use.

The principle from *Roberts v Roberts* [1970] P. 1, although old, remains good law. It was set out and approved by the court in *Vaughan v Vaughan* [2010] EWCA Civ 349 as follows, per Wilson LJ at [37-38]:

> 'The court (Sir Jocelyn Simon P and Rees J) [in *Roberts*]
>
> (a) decided, at 3E, to survey the relevance not only of a husband's moral obligation to support a cohabitant but also of an ex-husband's legal obligation to support a second wife (on the basis that the claim of the former could not rank higher than that of the latter);
>
> (b) held, at 6E to 8B, that not only an ex-husband's legal obligation to a second wife but also a moral obligation of a husband or ex-husband to a cohabitant had to be brought into account in assessing the level of his obligation to maintain a first wife; but
>
> (c) held, at 8G, that "on general principle, a spouse must on marriage be presumed … to take the other subject to all existing encumbrances,

whether known or not – for example ... an obligation to support the wife or child of a dissolved marriage"; but

(d) considered, at 8H to 9F, that English law did not, as did some Commonwealth courts, take the principle to its logical conclusion by affording "primacy" or "priority" to the claims of the first wife; yet nevertheless

(e) concluded, at 5D and 10D, that a decision, such as that of the justices, to give such "priority" to the claims of the cohabitant (or second wife) as virtually to ignore the claims of the first wife was plainly wrong.

Any judge-made "principle" of family law enunciated over forty years ago requires rigorous scrutiny in case changed social conditions have rendered it obsolete. But I see no reason to conclude (and Mr Mostyn did not argue) that the principle enunciated in the case of *Roberts* and quoted at [37(c)] is obsolete. It has been applied in a few reported cases, albeit themselves also now old, and it remains in the textbooks. But what was and is its effect? In the interests of realism and practicality the Divisional Court muffled it. And, to the muffling of it, we should certainly still subscribe. One may conclude with confidence only that the court should always have the principle in mind; that it should give effect to it where it reasonably can; and that, although it should not go so far as to give priority to the claims of the first wife, it should certainly not give priority to the claims of the second wife.'

The other helpful authority on this topic is *Cameron-Webb v Cameron-Webb (No 2)* [1982] 3 FLR 389, which provides guidance about how practically to proceed where there are two, likely competing, spouses with live claims.

The court in *Cameron-Webb* held that when considering wife/spouse one's application for financial provision, section 25 MCA required the court to take into account the actual and foreseeable obligations of the husband – and so to take into account the position of the wife/spouse two too, and the husband's obligations towards her. The FLR summary states:

> 'If the applications were heard separately the court might have to rely on evidence which was untested by one party, the husband or his accountants might give differing evidence at each hearing, matters relevant to one application might come to light in the other, and the court might be driven to reach different values.
>
> The wives' interests were similar and the husband's assets were substantial enough to avoid putting the wives in an adversarial position as between themselves. In any event such a possible conflict must be weighed against the duty of the court under s.25 of the 1973 Act and the need to do justice between the husband and each wife. It would be impossible to decide what was fair, just and reasonable between the husband and each wife unless the evidence was considered in its entirety. Accordingly, the two applications would be consolidated.'

CHAPTER SIX

CONCLUSION

We hope this Guide will allow remarriages to be celebrated without stressful legal stings. Remarriages are, after all, 'a triumph of hope over experience' (according to Samuel Johnson in the eighteenth-century).

When section 28(3) MCA was first being considered and drafted, the Law Commission's reasoning reveals an interesting angle. In July 1969[8], The Law Commission said: 'A wife who has gone through a form of marriage with a second "husband" should not, in our view, be entitled to revive her rights against her first husband by having her second "marriage" annulled. If the annulment is in England, the English courts have power to order financial provision from the second "husband". If it is in a foreign country, the courts of that country may not have that power, and she may be left without rights against either husband. But in our view, the principle must be that once another marriage has been contracted, that destroys any claim against a former spouse.'[9]

The gender-based assumptions and stereotypes that appear throughout the Law Commission's recommendations on this topic are conspicuously out-of-date to the present-day reader.

Section 28(3) MCA was certainly more relevant in the days when a remarried wife was seen as her new husband's responsibility. Has the

8 The Law Commission, Law Com No. 25, Report on financial provision in matrimonial proceedings, 24 July 1969.

9 Paragraph 14, Law Com No. 25 Report.

elephant trap created by section 28(3) now become obsolete, as such attitudes fade?

When section 28(3) MCA does bite, the sharing principle can be completely undermined. Does this consequence remain appropriate today?

It will be interesting to see how this subject develops.

MORE BOOKS BY LAW BRIEF PUBLISHING

A selection of our other titles available now:-

'A Practical Guide to the Independent School Standards – September 2023 Edition' by Sarah McKimm
'A Practical Guide to Estate Administration and Crypto Assets' by Richard Marshall
'A Practical Guide to Managing GDPR Data Subject Access Requests – Second Edition' by Patrick O'Kane
'A Practical Guide to Parental Alienation in Private and Public Law Children Cases' by Sam King QC & Frankie Shama
'Contested Heritage – Removing Art from Land and Historic Buildings' by Richard Harwood QC, Catherine Dobson, David Sawtell
'The Limits of Separate Legal Personality: When Those Running a Company Can Be Held Personally Liable for Losses Caused to Third Parties Outside of the Company' by Dr Mike Wilkinson
'A Practical Guide to Transgender Law' by Robin Moira White & Nicola Newbegin
'A Practical Guide to 'Stranded Spouses' in Family Law' by Mani Singh Basi
'A Practical Guide to Residential Freehold Conveyancing' by Lorraine Richardson
'A Practical Guide to Pensions on Divorce for Lawyers' by Bryan Scant
'A Practical Guide to Challenging Sham Marriage Allegations in Immigration Law' by Priya Solanki
'A Practical Guide to Digital Communications Evidence in Criminal Law' by Sam Willis
'A Practical Guide to Legal Rights in Scotland' by Sarah-Jane Macdonald
'A Practical Guide to New Build Conveyancing' by Paul Sams & Rebecca East
'A Practical Guide to Defending Barristers in Disciplinary Cases' by Marc Beaumont
'A Practical Guide to Inherited Wealth on Divorce' by Hayley Trim
'A Practical Guide to Practice Direction 12J and Domestic Abuse in Private Law Children Proceedings' by Rebecca Cross & Malvika Jaganmohan

'A Practical Guide to Confiscation and Restraint'
by Narita Bahra QC, John Carl Townsend, David Winch

'A Practical Guide to the Law of Forests in Scotland' by Philip Buchan

'A Practical Guide to Health and Medical Cases in Immigration Law'
by Rebecca Chapman & Miranda Butler

'A Practical Guide to Bad Character Evidence for Criminal Practitioners
by Aparna Rao

'A Practical Guide to Extradition Law post-Brexit' by Myles Grandison et al

'A Practical Guide to Hoarding and Mental Health for Housing Lawyers'
by Rachel Coyle

'A Practical Guide to Psychiatric Claims in Personal Injury – 2nd Edition'
by Liam Ryan

'Stephens on Contractual Indemnities' by Richard Stephens

'A Practical Guide to the EU Succession Regulation' by Richard Frimston

'A Practical Guide to Solicitor and Client Costs – 2nd Edition' by Robin Dunne

'Constructive Dismissal – Practice Pointers and Principles' by Benjimin Burgher

'A Practical Guide to Religion and Belief Discrimination Claims in the Workplace'
by Kashif Ali

'A Practical Guide to the Law of Medical Treatment Decisions' by Ben Troke

'Fundamental Dishonesty and QOCS in Personal Injury Proceedings: Law and Practice' by Jake Rowley

'A Practical Guide to the Law in Relation to School Exclusions'
by Charlotte Hadfield & Alice de Coverley

'A Practical Guide to Divorce for the Silver Separators' by Karin Walker

'The Right to be Forgotten – The Law and Practical Issues' by Melissa Stock

'A Practical Guide to Planning Law and Rights of Way in National Parks, the Broads and AONBs' by James Maurici QC, James Neill et al

'A Practical Guide to Election Law' by Tom Tabori

'A Practical Guide to the Law in Relation to Surrogacy' by Andrew Powell

'A Practical Guide to Claims Arising from Fatal Accidents – 2nd Edition'
by James Patience

'A Practical Guide to the Ownership of Employee Inventions – From Entitlement to Compensation' by James Tumbridge & Ashley Roughton

'A Practical Guide to Asbestos Claims' by Jonathan Owen & Gareth McAloon

'A Practical Guide to Stamp Duty Land Tax in England and Northern Ireland' by Suzanne O'Hara
'A Practical Guide to the Law of Farming Partnerships' by Philip Whitcomb
'Covid-19, Homeworking and the Law – The Essential Guide to Employment and GDPR Issues' by Forbes Solicitors
'Covid-19 and Criminal Law – The Essential Guide' by Ramya Nagesh
'Covid-19 and Family Law in England and Wales – The Essential Guide' by Safda Mahmood
'A Practical Guide to the Law of Unlawful Eviction and Harassment – 2nd Edition' by Stephanie Lovegrove
'Covid-19, Brexit and the Law of Commercial Leases – The Essential Guide' by Mark Shelton
'A Practical Guide to Costs in Personal Injury Claims – 2nd Edition' by Matthew Hoe
'A Practical Guide to the General Data Protection Regulation (GDPR) – 2nd Edition' by Keith Markham
'Ellis on Credit Hire – Sixth Edition' by Aidan Ellis & Tim Kevan
'A Practical Guide to Working with Litigants in Person and McKenzie Friends in Family Cases' by Stuart Barlow
'Protecting Unregistered Brands: A Practical Guide to the Law of Passing Off' by Lorna Brazell
'A Practical Guide to Secondary Liability and Joint Enterprise Post-Jogee' by Joanne Cecil & James Mehigan
'A Practical Guide to the Pre-Action RTA Claims Protocol for Personal Injury Lawyers' by Antonia Ford
'A Practical Guide to Neighbour Disputes and the Law' by Alexander Walsh
'A Practical Guide to Forfeiture of Leases' by Mark Shelton
'A Practical Guide to Coercive Control for Legal Practitioners and Victims' by Rachel Horman
'A Practical Guide to the Law of Driverless Cars – Second Edition' by Alex Glassbrook, Emma Northey & Scarlett Milligan
'A Practical Guide to TOLATA Claims' by Greg Williams
'A Practical Guide to Elderly Law – 2nd Edition' by Justin Patten
'A Practical Guide to Responding to Housing Disrepair and Unfitness Claims' by Iain Wightwick

'A Practical Guide to the Law of Bullying and Harassment in the Workplace' by Philip Hyland
'How to Be a Freelance Solicitor: A Practical Guide to the SRA-Regulated Freelance Solicitor Model' by Paul Bennett
'A Practical Guide to Prison Injury Claims' by Malcolm Johnson
'A Practical Guide to the Small Claims Track – 2nd Edition' by Dominic Bright
'A Practical Guide to Advising Clients at the Police Station' by Colin Stephen McKeown-Beaumont
'A Practical Guide to Antisocial Behaviour Injunctions' by Iain Wightwick
'Practical Mediation: A Guide for Mediators, Advocates, Advisers, Lawyers, and Students in Civil, Commercial, Business, Property, Workplace, and Employment Cases' by Jonathan Dingle with John Sephton
'The Mini-Pupillage Workbook' by David Boyle
'A Practical Guide to Crofting Law' by Brian Inkster
'A Practical Guide to the Law of Domain Names and Cybersquatting' by Andrew Clemson
'A Practical Guide to the Law of Gender Pay Gap Reporting' by Harini Iyengar
'NHS Whistleblowing and the Law' by Joseph England
'Employment Law and the Gig Economy' by Nigel Mackay & Annie Powell
'A Practical Guide to Noise Induced Hearing Loss (NIHL) Claims' by Andrew Mckie, Ian Skeate, Gareth McAloon
'An Introduction to Beauty Negligence Claims – A Practical Guide for the Personal Injury Practitioner' by Greg Almond
'Intercompany Agreements for Transfer Pricing Compliance' by Paul Sutton
'Zen and the Art of Mediation' by Martin Plowman
'A Practical Guide to the SRA Principles, Individual and Law Firm Codes of Conduct 2019 – What Every Law Firm Needs to Know' by Paul Bennett
'A Practical Guide to Adoption for Family Lawyers' by Graham Pegg
'A Practical Guide to Industrial Disease Claims' by Andrew Mckie & Ian Skeate
'A Practical Guide to Conducting a Sheriff Court Proof' by Andrew Stevenson
'A Practical Guide to Vicarious Liability' by Mariel Irvine
'A Practical Guide to Applications for Landlord's Consent and Variation of Leases' by Mark Shelton
'A Practical Guide to Relief from Sanctions Post-Mitchell and Denton' by Peter Causton

'A Practical Guide to Equity Release for Advisors' by Paul Sams

'A Practical Guide to Financial Services Claims' by Chris Hegarty

'The Law of Houses in Multiple Occupation: A Practical Guide to HMO Proceedings' by Julian Hunt

'Occupiers, Highways and Defective Premises Claims: A Practical Guide Post-Jackson – 2nd Edition' by Andrew Mckie

'A Practical Guide to Financial Ombudsman Service Claims' by Adam Temple & Robert Scrivenor

'A Practical Guide to Running Housing Disrepair and Cavity Wall Claims: 2nd Edition' by Andrew Mckie & Ian Skeate

'A Practical Guide to Holiday Sickness Claims – 2nd Edition' by Andrew Mckie & Ian Skeate

'Arguments and Tactics for Personal Injury and Clinical Negligence Claims' by Dorian Williams

'A Practical Guide to Drone Law' by Rufus Ballaster, Andrew Firman, Eleanor Clot

'A Practical Guide to Compliance for Personal Injury Firms Working With Claims Management Companies' by Paul Bennett

'RTA Allegations of Fraud in a Post-Jackson Era: The Handbook – 2nd Edition' by Andrew Mckie

'RTA Personal Injury Claims: A Practical Guide Post-Jackson' by Andrew Mckie

'On Experts: CPR35 for Lawyers and Experts' by David Boyle

'An Introduction to Personal Injury Law' by David Boyle

These books and more are available to order online direct from the publisher at www.lawbriefpublishing.com, where you can also read free sample chapters. For any queries, contact us on 0844 587 2383 or mail@lawbriefpublishing.com.

Our books are also usually in stock at www.amazon.co.uk with free next day delivery for Prime members, and at good legal bookshops such as Wildy & Sons.

We are regularly launching new books in our series of practical day-to-day practitioners' guides. Visit our website and join our free newsletter to be kept informed and to receive special offers, free chapters, etc.

You can also follow us on Twitter at www.twitter.com/lawbriefpub.

www.ingramcontent.com/pod-product-compliance
Lightning Source LLC
LaVergne TN
LVHW022312200926
848481LV00004B/1296
* 9 7 8 1 9 1 6 6 9 8 4 3 7 *